A PLAY FOR ALL

Meish Goldish
Illustrated by Jeff Hopkins

Rigby®
A Harcourt Achieve Imprint

www.Rigby.com
1-800-531-5015

Our class was learning about **rights** and **responsibilities**.

A **right** is something that you are free to do. A **responsibility** is something that you should do.

3

We wrote a play
about what we had learned.
Everyone in the class
had a part in the play.

A Play for All

Characters

 Drew   Bart

 Amy   Carla

 Fred    Terry

 Cris   Sara

Setting

Our classroom

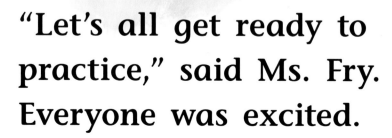

"Let's all get ready to practice," said Ms. Fry. Everyone was excited.

Bart wasn't sure about the play. "I'd rather just watch," said Bart.

Ms. Fry said, "That's fine.
You may watch the play
and join in when you're ready."

Ms. Fry asked the students
to get the props ready.
Fred and Amy made posters.
Carla found a few balls.
Terry looked for a jump rope.

"Okay class,
it looks like we are ready.
Take your places
and let's start the play!"
said Ms. Fry.

We have rights!

FRED: We're free to read
the books we like.

CRIS: We're free to skate or ride a bike.

DREW: We're free to go
to school each day.

CARLA: We're free to choose what sport to play.

TERRY: We're free to do what we choose.

SARA: We're free to wear our dancing shoes.

SARA: We should play fair in a game.

CARLA: We should treat all people the same.

AMY: We should vote
for someone to lead.

DREW: We should vote
for something we need.

Bart jumped up and said,
"This play is great!
I should do my part."

"I'm glad you chose to join in,
Bart," said Ms. Fry.
"You always have the right
to change your mind."

"Great job on the play, class!"
said Ms. Fry.

"Now, who can tell me what we mean by rights and responsibilities?"

Bart smiled and raised his hand.

"I have the right
to sometimes be shy,
and the responsibility
to give things a try!"